ANIMALS ON THE EDGE

PENGUIN

21

ANIMALS ON THE EDGE

PENGUIN

by Anna Claybourne

BLOOMSBURY

LONDON BERLIN NEW YORK SYDNEY

Published 2012 by
Bloomsbury Publishing Plc
50 Bedford Square, London, WC1B 3DP

www.bloomsbury.com

ISBN HB 978-1-4081-4822-8
ISBN PB 978-1-4081-4960-7

Picture acknowledgements:
Cover: Shutterstock
Insides: All Shutterstock except for the following; p8 bottom ©Melanie Conner (National Science Foundation) via Wikimedia Commons, p9 right inset ©Nobu Tamura (own work) via Wikimedia Commons, p10 top inset ©Herbert George Ponting via Wikimedia Commons, page 10 bottom ©IFAW, p11 top ©ZSL, p14 top ©ZSL, p14 bottom ©The Royal Zoological Society of Scotland, p15 top ©R Kellehar, p15 bottom ©W J Harrison via Flickr Commons, p17 centre ©ZSL, pp18-19 all images ©ZSL, p21 left inset ©ZSL/Michael Lyster, p22 top ©E Jenner, p22 bottom ©ZSL, p23 bottom ©Hagen Hopkins, via Getty Images News, pp24-25 central image ©Eli Duke via Flickr Commons, p27 bottom ©Alan Lewis, p28 top inset ©ZSL/Evelyn Guyett, p28 bottom inset ©Liam Quinn via Flickr Creative Commons, p29 top inset ©Commonwealth of Australia/Gavin Johnstone, p29 bottom inset ©Liam Quinn via Flickr Creative Commons, p32 ©S Isle, p33 bottom inset ©Emily Colin, Pedal.For.Change, pedalforchangeenvironmentaljustice. blogspot.com, p34 all images ©ZSL/Evelyn Guyett, p35 top ©ZSL/Evelyn Guyett, p35 bottom ©Liam Quinn via Flickr Creative Commons, pp36-37 central ©ZSL, p37 ©ZSL, p38 top inset ©Commonwealth of Australia 2011, p41 bottom inset ©ZSL/Tom Hart

Manufactured and supplied under licence from the Zoological Society of London.

Produced for Bloomsbury Publishing Plc by Geoff Ward.

A CIP catalogue for this book is available from the British Library.

Printed in China by C&C Offset Printing Co.

CONTENTS

MEET THE PENGUINS

Penguins are birds – but very unusual ones! They can't fly, and they have short, stubby legs, so they waddle around, rocking from side to side. But under the water, penguins are fast and graceful. They dive into the sea and zoom to and fro, using their wings and webbed feet as flippers.

How many penguins?

There are around 20 different types, or **species**, of penguins. They range from the fairy penguin, at just 40cm tall, to the emperor penguin, which can grow to be up to 120cm. All penguins are a similar shape, and mostly black and white. But some have patches of orange or yellow, or sticking-up feather **crests** on their heads.

A Humboldt penguin, from South America, glides along under the water.

BIRDS OF THE SOUTH

Penguins are famous for living on the icy shores of Antarctica, the huge, freezing cold continent around the South Pole. But not all types of penguins are found there. Some actually live in much warmer places, such as Australia, Africa, and even the Galapagos Islands, very close to the **equator**. However, you'll only find wild penguins in the southern **hemisphere** – the southern half of the Earth.

The yellow areas on this map show where penguins live in the wild.

Penguins in peril

It's not always easy being a penguin. In some places, their icy homes are melting, and they are running out of fish to eat. They are at risk from hunting, **pollution** (such as oil spills) and disease. Some penguin species are in danger of dying out, and others could be soon. This book explains why they are at risk, and how we can help them.

Rockhopper penguin

Chinstrap penguin

Fairy penguin

DID YOU KNOW?

Some of the first explorers to see penguins thought that they were fish, as they are such good swimmers and have a **streamlined**, fishy shape.

PENGUINS ON THE EDGE

Penguins are brilliantly adapted, or suited, to one way of living. But if things change, they can struggle to survive. And, thanks to humans, things are changing a lot.

Problems for penguins

Here are some of the problems facing penguins:

- **Global warming** The Earth is gradually heating up, and ice is melting – so many penguins' habitats (natural homes) are changing.
- **Fishing** We catch so much fish that fish-eating wild animals, such as penguins, can suffer from food shortages.
- **Disease** Penguins can catch deadly diseases, sometimes from humans.
- **Pollution** Oil spills in the sea, and other types of pollution, can kill penguins or make them ill.
- **Hunting** Humans often hunted penguins in the past, and a lot of other animals hunt them too.

WHO EATS PENGUINS?

Penguins are a popular food for large sea creatures, like sharks, leopard seals and killer whales. On land, they are also eaten by foxes, eagles, ferrets, wild cats, and even some snakes.

This skua, a large hunting bird, is trying to scare an Adélie penguin off its nest in order to steal its egg.

Which penguins?

The IUCN, or International Union for the Conservation of Nature, keeps records of living things and their **conservation status** – whether they are at risk of dying out. Some penguins are more endangered than others.

Vulnerable – penguins likely to become endangered:

Southern rockhopper penguin
Humboldt penguin
Macaroni penguin
Royal penguin
Snares penguin

Endangered – penguins at risk of dying out:

Galapagos penguin
Yellow-eyed penguin
Erect-crested penguin
Northern rockhopper penguin
Fiordland penguin
Black-footed or African penguin

Near threatened – penguins that could become endangered soon:

Gentoo penguin
Magellanic penguin

The waimanu is one of the many species of penguins that are now extinct. It lived around 60 million years ago.

The yellow-eyed penguin mainly lives around New Zealand's South Island, where it nests on coastlines among trees or bushes. There is only a small area of natural habitat left for it.

PREHISTORIC PENGUINS

Fossils show that millions of years ago, giant penguins lived in what is now Peru. Some were as tall as a human! One, known as the water king, had an amazingly long, sharp beak, too.

WE LOVE PENGUINS!

"We saw the little Adélie penguins hurrying to meet us… They are extraordinarily like children, these little people of the Antarctic world. We used to sing to them, as they to us." Antarctic explorer Apsley Cherry-Garrard.

Cute and funny

The words of explorer Apsley Cherry-Garrard sum up how most people feel about penguins. They appeal to us, and often seem almost human. It could be because of the way they stand upright, and waddle like toddlers, or the way they love to play and explore. Penguins are also known for being curious and friendly towards humans.

Apsley Cherry-Garrard went to Antarctica as part of a team led by Captain Robert Scott in 1910, partly to study penguins. Four of the team died, but Cherry-Garrard survived and wrote a book about his adventures.

Getting oil on their feathers means penguins can't keep warm or catch fish, and soon die if they are not cleaned.

THE TREASURE DISASTER

In the year 2000, the *Treasure* cargo ship sank off South Africa, and leaked fuel oil into the sea. It surrounded two islands where endangered black-footed penguins live, and thousands of them were covered in oil. Hundreds and hundreds of **volunteers** came from South Africa, and around the world, to help collect, clean up and care for the penguins.

Popular penguins

Of course, this doesn't actually mean penguins *are* much like people. They are no more similar to us than a crow, a chicken, or any other bird. But people feel caring towards them – and that's good news for conservation. Penguins are popular in zoos, and people don't like to think of them dying out in the wild. So they are keen to help save penguin species.

A visitor gets a great view of penguins underwater at ZSL London Zoo's Penguin Beach.

PENGUINS IN THE MOVIES

There have been several big box-office films about penguins, including the animated film Happy Feet, and March of the Penguins. As well as telling a story, they help us learn more about how penguins live and the problems they have.

Penguins everywhere!

Look around, and you'll see penguins popping up on all kinds of everyday objects, from books to chocolate bars. They're in adverts, cartoons and children's songs. There are penguin cards, games and cuddly toys – all showing how much we like having them around.

Cute plastic penguins ready to be hooked in a fairground game.

PENGUINS AT HOME

In the wild, all penguins live around coasts. They swim in the sea to catch fish, but go onto the land to lay their eggs, hatch them and look after their chicks.

Cold water

Penguins live either in very cold places, such as Antarctica, or in warmer places that have cold water **currents**. A current is a flow of water, a bit like a river, but in the sea, not on land. For example, the cold Humboldt current flows up the west coast of South America, and this is where Humboldt and Magellanic penguins live. Cold water has more fish and other animals living in it, providing food for penguins.

Pressing their bodies together keeps heat in, and helps penguins not to freeze.

DID YOU KNOW?

All penguins are **countershaded** – mainly black on the back, and white on the front. This looks striking to us, but when a penguin is swimming in the sea, its underside is in shadow, and the sun shines on its back. The countershading disguises the shadow, making penguins harder for **predators** to spot.

Penguins mainly swim flat on their stomachs, like ducks.

Super-swimmers

Though they can't fly in the air, penguins use their wings to "fly" underwater. They swoop, soar and glide through the ocean as they chase prey such as fish and squid, and speed away from hunters like seals and sharks. Some species, such as gentoos and black-footed penguins, can swim at 35km/h, as fast as a tiger can run.

Instead of climbing out of the sea, penguins can zoom up out of the water and jump right onto the land.

Penguins on land

When they're not in the water, penguins live on land, or on solid ice. In the icy Antarctic, they can get around quickly on the ice by **tobogganing** – sliding along on their stomachs. Some penguins live in large groups, or **colonies**, and huddle together to keep warm. Some, especially in warmer areas, dig burrows in the ground to hide in, or make nests under bushes.

Penguins slide along on their stomachs to save energy.

PENGUINS IN THE ZOO

If you go to visit a zoo, there's a very good chance it will have penguins. Penguins have been living in zoos for many years, and most species seem to be happy there.

A perfect penguin pad

Penguins like living together, so most zoos have a group of penguins, not just one. They often keep several different species in the same **enclosure**. The enclosure must have a pool that's big enough for the penguins to swim in, and a large area of land too. Each species needs its own type of ground surface – for example, rocks or concrete for Adélie penguins, grass and soil for black-footed penguins, and rock or ice for emperor penguins.

Zookeepers make notes about the penguins they look after, keeping a record of their health and habits.

SIR NILS OLAV

Sir Nils Olav is a king penguin living at Edinburgh Zoo. He is the official **mascot** of the King's Guard of Norway, part of Norway's army. The King's Guard has visited him several times, and even awarded him a knighthood! He is actually the second Nils Olav, as the first one died in 1987.

Nils Olav inspects the troops during a ceremony at Edinburgh Zoo.

The penguins at Penguin Beach admiring their new pool and pebbly shore.

Keeping cool

Some penguin species could easily get too hot in a zoo in a warm or hot country. Antarctic penguins like Adélies and emperors need the temperature to be kept close to freezing. They might have chunks of ice to stand on, refrigerated floors, or whole **refrigerated** rooms where they can cool down. Some zoos have cold water sprinklers and fountains for the penguins too.

Penguin Beach

Penguin Beach is a modern penguin enclosure at ZSL London Zoo. It was built to replace the old penguin enclosure with a bigger, better and more natural penguin home. It's home to lots of Humboldt penguins and one rockhopper penguin. It has several different land areas for the different species, and its pool is kept salty, like the sea.

Bubbles of air escape from this king penguin's mouth and feathers as it takes an underwater swim.

THE LIVING COAST

At some zoos, like ZSL London Zoo, San Francisco Zoo and Brookfield Zoo in Chicago, you can watch the penguins under the water, through a glass window in the side of their pool.

PENGUIN FOOD

Penguins eat fish and other sea creatures, especially squid, octopuses and krill, a type of shrimp. They can dive as deep as 500m underwater to chase prey, and have very good eyesight for spotting it in the murky depths.

Going hunting

To catch a fish or other food, a penguin zooms after it and grabs it in its beak. A penguin's tongue has backward-pointing spikes on it, which help it get a firm grip on wriggling, slithery fish or squid. Then the penguin gulps its prey down whole. It dissolves into mush in the penguin's stomach. An emperor penguin, the biggest penguin, usually eats 2-3kg of food each day. If it's very hungry and needs to get fatter, it can eat up to 6kg – almost half the penguin's own weight!

DO PEOPLE EAT PENGUINS?

Eating penguins is rare now, and it's **illegal** to hunt them. But long ago, sailors used to eat them, and so did Antarctic explorers – even though they weren't very nice to eat. They were said to taste like gone-off, fishy-flavoured chicken.

A penguin uses its beak to jerk a fish into the right position, before swallowing it whole.

In the zoo

Zoo penguins are usually fed twice a day, while the zoo is open so that visitors can watch. The keepers bring the penguins buckets of fish, which are dead, not alive! They either feed each penguin by hand, or throw the bucketful of fish into the water for the penguins to dive after.

PENGUIN FOOD SHOPPING LIST

Penguins aren't fussy, and don't need many different kinds of food. A typical zoo's shopping list for its penguins is pretty simple:

- Two big boxes of capelin fish per day
- **Vitamin** tablets

A keeper feeds the penguins by hand, giving each one its own fish.

WHY ARE PENGUINS SMELLY?

In the zoo, you can sometimes smell the penguin enclosure before you see it. This is because penguins have smelly poo! They eat a lot of fish, and their poo comes out smelling fishy too. The keepers have to clean up the penguin poo every day.

From top: capelin, sardines and krill, all favourite foods for penguins.

A DAY IN THE LIFE: PENGUIN KEEPER

Zuzana Matyasova is a penguin keeper at ZSL London Zoo's Penguin Beach. She describes a day working with the penguins, and what they're like when you get to know them!

Zuzana is never far from a penguin when she's at work at ZSL London Zoo.

Daily diary

8.00am In the morning, two of us go over to the penguin enclosure. We check everything looks OK and that the fence is in good shape. Then we make sure all the penguins are accounted for and healthy.

9.30am It's time to open up the Penguin Beach exhibit, ready for the public. Once it's open, we get to work on cleaning jobs – cleaning all the windows, scrubbing the rocks, and cleaning the pool, using a special hoover to suck out penguin poo and uneaten fish.

11.00am The next job is to prepare the penguins' food. I put vitamin tablets into the fish, then get the buckets of fish ready.

Penguins don't want to swim in a dirty pool – so it has to be cleaned out every day.

12.00pm We sometimes give the penguins some kind of **enrichment**, or fun things for them to do. If it's hot, they enjoy a "fish ice bucket" – a bucket of water filled with fish, frozen solid and then tipped out onto the ground. It's like a giant fishy ice lolly.

2.30pm We take two buckets of fish into the enclosure for the penguins' first feeding session. We usually throw the fish into the pool, and the penguins chase after it.

4.30pm The penguins get their second meal of the day. If we have visitors coming into the enclosure for a "meet the penguins" experience, they sometimes help to feed them. The penguins love to interact with keepers and visitors.

The fish have to be prepared with added vitamins before feeding time.

DO ALL THE PENGUINS HAVE NAMES?

Most of the penguins don't actually have their own names – they have wing tags with numbers so we can tell them apart. But we have named a few, such as Egg and Cake, the two young Humboldt penguins, and Ricky the rockhopper.

Penguins like to investigate everything around them. This Humboldt penguin is interested in the keeper's clipboard.

Penguin personalities

The penguins are very playful. I've seen some of them chasing wasps and butterflies around the enclosure. Whenever we do any kind of glass cleaning, they come and follow the movements of the sponge on the glass and try to catch it. And when we hoover the bottom of the pool, they come and play with the hoover handle.

In fact, whenever we do any kind of work in the enclosure, the penguins like to come and run around with us. The two **juvenile** Humboldt penguins also peck at our legs when we're doing public talks!

PENGUIN CHICKS

To breed and have chicks, a male and a female penguin have to get together to mate. In most species, the males do a courtship display to attract a female. They call loudly, make bobbing or waving movements, and start finding places to nest. The females choose the males they like best!

Eggs and nests

Penguins lay eggs, like all birds. But they don't all make nests. Emperor penguins breed on the Antarctic ice, where the eggs would freeze. So each male balances his egg on his feet, and covers it with his stomach. While he waits for the egg to hatch, the mother penguin goes to the sea to feed.

Adélie penguins make their nests from piles of pebbles, while rockhoppers use grass, twigs and feathers. Fairy penguins lay their eggs in burrows close to the shore.

A fluffy emperor penguin chick keeps warm under its dad's stomach.

This Adélie penguin has found a perfect stone to add to its nest.

Fluffy chicks

Wherever they nest, both penguin parents help to look after their chicks. Before the chicks can swim and catch their own food, the parents catch fish for them. They come back from the sea and **regurgitate** (cough up) fish from their stomachs to feed their babies.

Newborn penguin chicks are soft and fluffy. As they grow, they lose their fluffy baby feathers and grow sleek, waterproof adult feathers.

This gentoo penguin mum is regurgitating some fishy mush into her baby's beak. When they return from the sea, penguin parents and chicks recognise each other by their calls.

Though he was raised by humans instead of his own parents, Dave is a healthy and happy penguin.

DAVE THE BLACK-FOOTED PENGUIN

Dave the black-footed penguin was born at ZSL London Zoo. His parents, Stuart and Stan (Stuart is the mum!) cared for their egg brilliantly, but when the chick hatched, they didn't look after him. So the keepers took over, fed and looked after the chick, and named him "Dave".

In the zoo

In zoos, the keepers give the penguins whatever they need for making their nests – twigs, leaves, pebbles, or sometimes special nesting boxes to use instead of a burrow. Penguins don't need much help to mate, as long as there are males and females in the enclosure. But the keepers do watch them carefully, and record which ones are breeding.

ONE PENGUIN'S STORY: RICKY THE ROCKHOPPER

Ricky the rockhopper penguin is one of the best-known penguins at ZSL London Zoo's Penguin Beach. He's the only rockhopper in the enclosure, and he knows he's a star!

Born in the country

Ricky hatched from his egg at ZSL Whipsnade Zoo in Bedfordshire, in 2008. As sometimes happens, his parents refused to care for him, so he was hand-reared. Once he was grown up, Ricky went to live at ZSL London Zoo, at the new Penguin Beach enclosure.

Ricky always likes to check out everything that's going on around him.

As he's a rockhopper, Ricky has long, yellow and black feather plumes above his eyes.

A colony of rockhopper penguins nesting on a steep slope by the sea in the Falkland Islands.

In the limelight

Ricky is a very popular penguin, loved by keepers and visitors alike. He's very friendly and loves to follow the keepers around. Or he goes over to wherever the biggest crowd of visitors are, and has a good look at them. He'll show off to whoever is watching! He likes to boss everyone around, including all the other penguins who live at Penguin Beach.

Rare rockhoppers

Ricky himself is a Northern rockhopper penguin – a rare and endangered species. They live in the southern Atlantic and Indian Oceans, on and around islands such as Gough and Tristan da Cunha. In 2011, a ship sank near Nightingale Island and leaked oil into the sea, surrounding the island and its rockhoppers. Some died, and the others had to be rescued and cleaned up.

This emperor penguin is being transported from New Zealand back to Antarctic waters.

ON THE MOVE

How do you move a penguin? The answer is carefully – especially species that like freezing weather. They are moved in an enclosed, refrigerated truck, with a layer of rocks and ice or snow in the bottom. The inside of the truck has a dim light switched on at all times to keep the penguins calm. To fly long distances, penguins can be carried on aeroplanes, each in its own ice-cooled kennel.

THREATS TO PENGUINS

Different penguins have to deal with different problems, depending on which species they are, and where they live. Even penguins that aren't at risk are still affected by some of these threats.

Melting ice

Global warming is now melting lots of Antarctic ice. Emperor males can only carry their eggs on their feet on flat, smooth ice. And krill, which some penguins eat, feed on creatures that live under ice. As more ice melts, penguins like Adélies and emperors will suffer.

Hot water

Cold water contains more **oxygen** than warm water. This means more fish and krill (which need oxygen) can live in it. But global warming is heating up the oceans, meaning less food for penguins.

Emperor penguins nest on ice sheets, which are now breaking up as the world gets warmer.

DID YOU KNOW?

Humboldt, rockhopper, Galapagos and several other types of penguins often die when they get caught in fishing nets.

Fighting for fish

Humans can catch a lot of fish at once, using hi-tech fishing gear. If we catch too much, penguins can run out of food. Krill fishing is one of the biggest threats, as it's becoming more common. We mainly catch krill to use as fish food on fish farms.

Diseases

Antarctica used to be a total **wilderness**, where people never went. But since we discovered it, penguins have been known to catch some diseases normally found in farm chickens. Scientists say they may have been spread from people's rubbish by other birds, such as **skuas**.

A fishing trawler in the chilly south Atlantic Ocean, where penguins depend on a good supply of fish.

Scientists are finding new ways to protect penguins.

Hunting

Hunting penguins is against the law now, but long ago, millions were killed for their meat, fat or other body parts. Explorers such as Ferdinand Magellan and his crew ate penguins when their food supplies ran out. Crews on whaling ships would catch thousands of penguins, and crush them to get their fat, which they used as a fuel.

New enemies

As humans have spread around the world, we've taken other animals with us, like rats, dogs and cats. They sometimes eat small penguins or their chicks, or steal their eggs. This could explain why penguins like rockhoppers are now so much rarer than they once were.

SPECIES IN DANGER

More than half of all penguin species are now officially endangered or threatened in some way. Here are just a few of them.

Black-footed or African penguin

Climate change and over-fishing have made it harder for black-footed penguins to find food. They've also been harmed by oil spills, and, in the past, by people taking their eggs to eat. In the last 100 years, the black-footed penguin **population** has fallen by 90 per cent.

Humboldt penguin

In the past, hunting and egg collecting harmed Humboldt penguins, which are found in South America (Peru and Chile). Today, they are threatened by over-fishing, oil spills, being caught in fishing nets, and warmer seas that contain less food. People also disturb the penguins' habitat to collect their **guano** (droppings), which is used as fertiliser.

HOW MANY PENGUINS?

No one knows exactly how many penguins there are altogether, but it's probably between 50 and 100 million. That sounds like a lot, but penguin populations have been dropping for years, and are still falling for many species. The rarest species are probably yellow-eyed and Galapagos penguins, with just a few thousands birds each.

King penguins can form huge breeding colonies of over 400,000 birds.

Yellow-eyed penguin

This is one of the most rare and endangered of all penguins. The seashore forests where it lives, in New Zealand, have mostly been turned into towns or farmland. Sharp-hoofed farm animals damage the penguins' nests, and they are hunted by rats, cats and dogs.

A yellow-eyed penguin on the lookout for danger in New Zealand.

Galapagos penguin

This penguin lives around the Galapagos Islands near the equator, further north than any other species. Huge numbers of them starve when climate change affects the cold-water currents that bring them food. They also get caught in fishing nets and hunted by wild cats, and suffer from a disease called avian malaria. It's spread by mosquitoes that came to the Galapagos Islands with humans in the 1980s.

A Galapagos penguin on the rocky beach in its warm, tropical home.

Erect-crested penguin

Not much is known about this crested penguin, which lives on islands around Australia and New Zealand. At least half the population has disappeared over the last 50 years, but scientists are not yet sure why. It could be to do with climate change, over-fishing or pollution.

As its name suggests, the erect-crested penguin's head feathers stick straight up.

PENGUIN LIFELINES

If they are going to survive, penguins urgently need a plan. So organisations all over the world have started conservation schemes to help them. Penguin Lifelines, which was founded by penguinologist Tom Hart from ZSL, is an example of a project that aims to find out the best ways to help Antarctic penguins – and to carry them out as soon as possible.

PENGUIN LIFELINES

Penguin science

Although penguins seem so familiar, there's still a lot we don't know about them. The Penguin Lifelines project sends scientists, zookeepers and volunteers to study penguins and collect **data** about them, so that we can learn more. They find out things like how many penguins each species has and where they live; how diseases affect them; where they go underwater and what they eat. They need to know these things in order to decide on the best conservation plans.

This is Tom Hart, who is a penguinologist – a scientist who studies penguins.

Port Lockroy in Antarctica, where scientists are testing what effect tourists have on penguin colonies.

Heading south

Penguin Lifelines focuses on the continent of Antarctica and the islands around it. On trips there, researchers mainly study king, Adélie, gentoo, chinstrap and Macaroni penguins. They go to the penguins' breeding areas, where they spend the most time on land. They **monitor** or keep track of the penguins, counting how big their colonies are, and how they react to climate change and fishing.

Spreading the word

Another important part of Penguin Lifelines is teaching the public about penguins and why they are at risk. People don't usually think of penguins as endangered species, or realise how things like fishing and climate change could affect them.

DID YOU KNOW?

Once in a while, a penguin is born that is all white or all black. A few, rare penguins have pale brown feathers where other penguins are black. When they are this colour they are called **Isabelline** penguins.

This Isabelline Royal penguin looks completely unlike the others in its colony.

MANY MACARONIS

There may be millions of Macaroni penguins, but we still need to worry about them. This is because like other penguin species, their population is **plummeting**. They face many threats: climate change, pollution, diseases, predators, and overfishing, especially of krill. They are found on many coasts and islands around Antarctica.

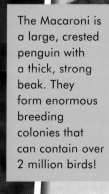

The Macaroni is a large, crested penguin with a thick, strong beak. They form enormous breeding colonies that can contain over 2 million birds!

PENGUIN-WATCHING

Penguins don't make it easy for scientists to study them! They live in remote, often freezing places, travel long distances and disappear underwater for long periods. A mission to monitor penguins in the Antarctic is a big challenge – it's freezing, windy, stormy, and can be dangerous.

Caught on camera

Researchers need to keep an eye on penguin colonies and what they get up to – but they can't live with the penguins permanently! Instead, they set up **time-lapse cameras**, on hillsides overlooking penguin breeding areas. The cameras take pictures three times a day, and send the information back to the scientists. They reveal when the breeding sites are busiest, and how the penguin colonies change over time.

A tourist stops to catch a beautiful emperor penguin on camera.

GETTING TO ANTARCTICA

When conservation workers go to the Antarctic, they usually fly to Argentina, in South America, and then travel by ship to the Antarctic coast or islands. To get from the ship onto the shore, they use small, inflatable "Zodiac" boats. If it's stormy or there are big waves, you can get cold and very wet!

DNA feather-printing

Scientists have come up with a great way to keep track of penguins and how they move around – **DNA feather-printing**. They collect penguin feathers from the ground, and note which colony each feather came from (penguins shed a lot of feathers after they breed).

Back in the lab, they can extract **DNA** from the feathers. DNA is stored in the cells of living things. Each species, and each individual penguin, has its own DNA patterns. So the feathers can reveal which penguins went where and how they are related to each other.

A Zodiac boat is a bit like a white-water rafting boat, and can carry about 12 people at a time.

A bigger boat like this lets you watch penguins at sea or on icebergs.

DO PENGUINS FALL OVER?

Since the 1980s, there has been a myth that penguins fall over when they look up to watch aircraft passing by. Scientists were worried that planes flying over Antarctica might be upsetting penguins and stopping them from breeding. So in 2000, a team of researchers went to test the theory out. They found that although penguins don't like the noise of aircraft, and waddle away when they fly too low, they do not fall over!

PENGUINS AND TOURISTS

It's fun seeing penguins in the zoo – so just imagine what it would be like to go to the Galapagos Islands, South Africa, or even Antarctica, to see them in the wild! Besides being exciting, going to see penguins in the wild can actually help them – as long as we do it carefully.

Fairy penguins at Phillip Island

There are several parts of the world where tourists can see wild penguins close-up. One is Phillip Island in Australia, home to thousands of fairy penguins, the smallest (and cutest!) penguins of all.

Tour organisers take visitors on trips to see the island's wildlife. In the evenings, when the fairy penguins come in from the sea to their burrows, the tourists can watch them from special viewing platforms, so as not to disturb them.

Please
CHECK UNDER YOUR CAR
Before driving away

TOURISTS IN ANTARCTICA

Scientists sometimes join tourist trips to Antarctica. It is a way for them to study penguins, and give wildlife talks for the passengers in return. They also collect tourists' photos of penguins, and use them as a way to keep track of where penguins are breeding.

A sign at Phillip Island warns visitors not to squash a penguin as they leave!

Ecotourism

Ecotourism means going to watch wildlife, or experience nature, as a holiday or leisure trip. It can be an important way to help endangered species, but it needs to be managed carefully.

How does it help?

- Ecotourism gives local people good jobs, and brings in money that can be used to pay for conservation projects.
- It makes people want to protect their wildlife and its habitat, as they are proud of it.
- Tourists seeing the wildlife learn about it, and want to save it too.

Why do we need to be careful?

- Visitors can harm habitats, by trampling plants, making noise, leaving litter or getting too close to wildlife.
- Tourists can bring in germs that spread to wild animals.
- Ecotourism often means building ticket offices, toilets, viewing platforms and pathways, and using transport that increases pollution. Too much of this can damage habitats too.

You can see this traveller's tour ship in the background as he goes ashore to photograph penguins.

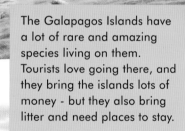

The Galapagos Islands have a lot of rare and amazing species living on them. Tourists love going there, and they bring the islands lots of money - but they also bring litter and need places to stay.

ONE PENGUIN'S STORY: THE LONELY MACARONI

Evelyn Guyett is a penguin keeper at ZSL London Zoo, who has also travelled to Antarctica to study wild penguins and collect their feathers for DNA feather-printing (see page 31). She tells the story of a penguin who seems to be slightly lost!

This is Evelyn Guyett, one of ZSL London Zoo's penguin keepers.

At home on Half Moon

Half Moon Island is a small, crescent-shaped island in the South Shetland Islands, near Antarctica. It's home to a breeding colony of six or seven thousand pairs of chinstrap penguins – and it's one of the places ZSL research trips go to collect penguin feathers.

The chinstraps are everywhere, but every year without fail, one lone Macaroni penguin joins the crowd. He is well known by all the expedition staff that revisit the island each summer. He can always be found perched on his favourite rock (unless he's out foraging). Macaronis typically nest further north, along the coastline of South Georgia. The lonely Macaroni is the only one spotted on Half Moon Island – he's never been seen with a mate.

The lonely Macaroni hangs out with some chinstrap friends on his favourite rock.

Who is the mysterious Macaroni?

While collecting feather samples from the chinstraps, we managed to catch the Macaroni quickly, and take a few feathers from him. Using these feathers, we can find out which Macaroni colony he's likely to have come from – and also whether he is, in fact, a boy, as I've been suggesting!

CHINSTRAPS AND MACARONIS

Chinstrap and Macaroni penguins are similar in size, but otherwise quite different. Macaronis, like rockhoppers and Royal penguins, are crested penguins, with sticking-up yellow feathers on their heads. Chinstraps are plain black and white, with a very clear, narrow "chinstrap" of black around their necks.

Though they are different species, the chinstraps and the Macaroni are happy to live side by side.

A group of Macaroni penguins patrol their zoo enclosure together.

CONSERVATION BREEDING

When you visit a penguin enclosure, you might be lucky enough to see penguin nests, eggs or fluffy chicks. Breeding animals in zoos helps us understand their wild cousins.

Why do it?

When a species is endangered, conservation breeding can help keep some animals alive and safe in zoos. It's also very useful to breed penguins in captivity, as it helps us learn so much more about how they have babies. Scientists can study things like how diseases affect breeding. This is very important, as penguin populations in the wild can only start to go up again by having lots of chicks.

A gentoo gets a head start with nest-building by using a specially made concrete nest.

STARS OF THE SHOW

Baby animals bring more visitors to zoos, because people love to see them. Newspapers often run reports about new chicks or other babies, too. The extra visitors raise awareness and money for the zoo's work.

Rockhopper couple Rita and Raef pose for the cameras at ZSL Whipsnade Zoo, UK.

Which species?

There are lots of penguin breeding schemes at zoos around the world. For example, Bristol Zoo UK, breeds black-footed or African penguins, and Edinburgh Zoo breeds rockhoppers and gentoos. Brookfield Zoo in Chicago, USA breeds Humboldt penguins, and organises Humboldt breeding around the world.

Working together

Zoos work together so that their penguins can breed with new mates and build up a healthy **captive** population. If the penguin keepers at one zoo find out something useful – like a good way to feed a chick – they will tell other zoos too, so that they can all look after their penguins as well as possible.

Soon after hatching, these gentoo penguin chicks at ZSL London Zoo are tiny, fluffy and super-cute!

RITA, RAEF AND WEBBER

Rita and Raef are a Northern rockhopper penguin pair living at ZSL Whipsnade Zoo. When rockhoppers mate, they usually stay together for life, and Rita and Raef love being together. In 2010, they had their first chick, named Webber! Webber had to be moved into his own special nursery room, as he kept wandering into the Humboldt penguins' area, and sometimes got pecked.

PROTECTED PLACES

Setting up protected areas can be a great way to protect endangered species and habitats. In these areas, no one is allowed to go fishing or hunting, use land for farming or building, or disturb wildlife.

Parks and reserves

There are various types of protected areas for wildlife, such as **national parks**, **nature reserves** and **coastal parks**. Some have fences around them, but often they just have laws to protect them, and **park rangers** to patrol them. Penguins need protected areas along the coast, extending into the sea. Here are some examples.

Macquarie Island Nature Reserve
World Heritage Area ⊗

An elephant seal in the Macquarie Island Nature Reserve. The land here is protected for wildlife.

MORE RESERVES

The **governments** of countries have to decide where to put nature reserves, and make sure there are strong laws to protect them. Wildlife conservation organisations can help them. They use the facts they find out about wildlife to show governments where protected areas should be, and what the wildlife there needs to survive. Argentina and some other countries around Antarctica are planning to open new protected areas soon.

Several species of penguins live on Kerguelen, including king penguins.

Patagonia and Monte Leon, Argentina

Argentina in South America is home to lots of penguins. It began opening coastal **marine** parks in 2004 to protect them, the fish they eat, and many other species.

Macquarie Island, Tasmania, Australia

Macquarie Island lies between Tasmania, southern Australia, and Antarctica. It is a marine reserve, protecting seals, albatrosses and other animals as well as several penguin species.

Kerguelen Islands, southern Indian Ocean

These islands, though close to Antarctica, are owned by France. They are part of a large nature reserve and science base. No one lives there except the scientists and the workers who run the science stations. This keeps the islands wild for the penguins.

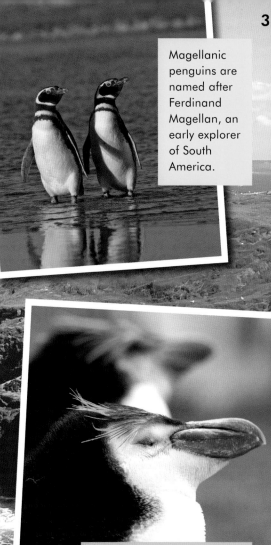

Magellanic penguins are named after Ferdinand Magellan, an early explorer of South America.

Macquarie Island is the only breeding site of the little-understood Royal penguin.

ANTARCTICA

Antarctica, the huge continent around the South Pole, does not belong to any one country. The countries of the world look after it together, and have agreed not to allow it to be used for mining, building or other development. It is kept as a natural habitat for wildlife, making it a kind of enormous nature reserve.

CAN WE SAVE THE PENGUINS?

If you went to Antarctica, and stood in the middle of a huge Adélie penguin breeding colony, you'd be surrounded by penguins as far as the eye can see. It wouldn't seem as if they might disappear. But the future for penguins really is very uncertain.

Are we helping?

Penguins do face a lot of different kinds of problems – but humans can definitely help to fix some of them. We can change our fishing habits, and make laws and nature reserves to protect penguins from danger. We can try to keep penguins from dying of disease. And we can change the way people see penguins. One hundred years ago, hunting penguins was pretty normal – today, it's very rare.

The return of the king

Scientists have also shown that penguin species can build up their numbers, if they get the chance. In the 1800s and 1900s, people hunted so many king penguins for their fat, skins and meat that their population crashed. After hunting was banned, king penguins have recovered well, and there are now over two million of them.

A busy Adélie penguin colony in Hope Bay, Antarctica.

Will penguins stay cool?

Unfortunately for penguins, one of their biggest problems is also one of the hardest to fix. The Earth's temperature is now rising faster than ever before in human history, and we don't really know how this will affect them. Some experts think it could actually wipe out most penguin species over the next 50-100 years. But the zoos, scientists and conservation workers aren't giving up the fight to save them.

Antarctic ice breaking up into sections during a warm spring.

King penguins at Hound Bay, Georgia, where ZSL have been studying them.

How can you help?

- **Adopt a penguin** Zoos often let you "adopt" animals. You pay to help look after them, and receive updates about them in return.
- **Try ecotourism** Maybe you could go on a penguin-watching trip on holiday, helping to raise money for conservation.
- **Go to the zoo** A trip to the zoo is another way to see penguins up close, and support conservation work.

- **Save the planet** Try to help stop global warming, by reducing car and plane travel and using less energy.
- **Be a penguinologist!** If you love penguins, you could even think about being a penguin scientist, keeper or conservation worker when you grow up. It will help to choose science subjects at school and college, especially biology.

ABOUT ZSL

The Zoological Society of London (ZSL) is a charity that provides conservation support for animals both in the UK and worldwide. We also run ZSL London Zoo and ZSL Whipsnade Zoo.

Our work in the wild extends to Antarctica, where our conservationists and scientists are working to give penguins a lifeline and protect them and their habitats for future generations.

By buying this book, you have helped us raise money to continue our conservation work with penguins and other animals in need of protection. Thank you.

To find out more about ZSL and how you can become further involved with our work visit **zsl.org**

Endangered penguins such as rockhoppers need help from conservation groups.

ZSL
LIVING CONSERVATION

ZSL LONDON ZOO

ZSL WHIPSNADE ZOO

Websites

Penguin Beach at London Zoo
www.zsl.org/penguinbeach

Penguin Beach Webcam
www.zsl.org/penguinwebcam

Adopt a Penguin
www.zsl.org/adoptapenguin

Penguin Lifelines
www.zsl.org/penguinlifelines

Places to visit

ZSL London Zoo
Outer Circle, Regent's Park, London,
NW1 4RY, UK
www.zsl.org/london
0844 225 1826

ZSL Whipsnade Zoo
Dunstable, Bedfordshire, LU6 2LF, UK
www.zsl.org/whipsnade
0844 225 1826

Helping penguins to breed as well as they can is vitally important.

Wild penguins deserve a safe, natural home where they can thrive.

GLOSSARY

adapt Change over time to suit the surroundings.

blog A kind of diary written on the Internet.

breed Mate and have babies.

captive breeding Breeding animals in zoos.

captivity Being kept in a zoo, wildlife park or garden.

climate The normal weather patterns in a particular place.

coastal park A national park or nature reserve covering a shoreline.

colony A group of animals, such as penguins, living together.

conservation Protecting nature and wildlife.

conservation status How endangered a particular species is.

continent One of the Earth's giant pieces of land.

countershading Dark colouring above and pale colouring below.

courtship display Dances or movements animals do to impress a mate.

crest Sticking-up feathers on a penguin's head.

current A flow of water through a sea, river or lake.

data Information.

DNA Short for deoxyribonucleic acid, a chemical found in body cells.

DNA feather-printing A way of finding out information about penguins from DNA in their feathers.

documentary A film about real-life events.

down Soft, fluffy inner feathers close to a bird's skin.

ecotourism Visiting wild places as a tourist to see wildlife.

EDGE Short for Evolutionarily Distinct and Globally Endangered.

enclosure A secure pen, cage or other home for a zoo animal.

endangered At risk of dying out and become extinct.

enrichment Entertainments and activities for zoo animals.

equator Imaginary line around the Earth, dividing it into north and south.

extinct No longer existing.

global warming Steady rise in the Earth's average temperature.

government The group of people in charge of a country.

guano Bird poo, especially when used as a fertiliser.

habitat The natural surroundings that a species lives in.

hemisphere Half of the globe.

illegal Against the law.

Isabelline penguin A penguin born with pale brown feathers where the black feathers normally are.

IUCN Short for the International Union for Conservation of Nature

juvenile Another word for young.

krill A type of shrimp.

marine To do with the seas and oceans.

monitor To check, measure or keep track of something.

national park A protected area of land where wildlife can live safely.

nature reserve A protected area of land where wildlife can live safely.

oxygen A gas found in the air, which animals need to breathe.

park ranger Someone who patrols and guards a national park.

penguinologist A penguin scientist.

plummet To fall incredibly quickly.

pollution Dirt or waste released into the surroundings.

population Number of people, or animals, in a particular place.

predator An animal that hunts and eats other animals.

prehistoric From a time before human history.

refrigerated Kept cool.

regurgitate To vomit up swallowed food for feeding a baby.

skua A type of seabird.

species A particular type of living thing.

status How endangered a living thing is.

streamlined Smoothly shaped to make it easier to move though air or water.

time-lapse camera A camera set to take pictures every few minutes or hours.

tobogganing The name for penguins sliding on their stomachs.

vitamins Chemicals that your body needs, found in some foods.

volunteer Someone who offers to do a job without being paid.

vulnerable At risk, but not as seriously as an endangered species.

wildlife reserve A protected area of land where wildlife can live safely.

ZSL Short for Zoological Society of London.

FIND OUT MORE

Books

A Day in the Life: Emperor Penguin by Katie Marsico, Raintree, 2011

Penguins: Discover More by Penny Arlon, Scholastic, 2012

Face-to-face with Penguins by Yva Momatiuk, National Geographic, 2010

Watching Penguins in Antarctica by Louise Spilsbury and Richard Spilsbury, Heinemann, 2007

100 Things You Should Know About Penguins by Camilla de la Bedoyere, Miles Kelly Publishing, 2010

Saving Wildlife: Polar Animals by Sonia Newland, Franklin Watts, 2010

What's it Like to be a... Zoo Keeper? by Elizabeth Dowen and Lisa Thompson, 2010

Websites

Humboldt Penguins at Brookfield Zoo
www.brookfieldzoo.org/czs/Humboldt

BBC penguin information, videos and sounds
Adélie penguin:
www.bbc.co.uk/nature/life/Adelie_Penguin

Emperor penguin:
www.bbc.co.uk/nature/life/Emperor_Penguin

Magellanic penguin:
www.bbc.co.uk/nature/life/Magellanic_Penguin

EDGE of Existence
www.edgeofexistence.org

Exodus
www.exodus.co.uk

Places to visit

Bristol Zoo Gardens
Clifton, Bristol, BS8 3HA, UK
www.bristolzoo.org.uk
0117 974 7399

Edinburgh Zoo
Corstorphine, Edinburgh, EH12 6TS, UK
www.edinburghzoo.org.uk/
0131 334 9171

Brookfield Zoo
8400 31st Street, Brookfield, IL 60513, Chicago, USA
www.brookfieldzoo.org

Phillip Island Nature Parks
895 Phillip Island Tourist Road,
Newhaven, Victoria 3925, Australia

INDEX

OTHER TITLES IN THE ANIMALS ON THE EDGE SERIES

www.storiesfromthezoo.com

Rhino
ISBN: HB 978-1-4081-4823-5
PB 978-1-4081-4956-0

Tiger
ISBN: HB 978-1-4081-4824-2
PB 978-1-4081-4957-7

Gorilla
ISBN: HB 978-1-4081-4825-9
PB 978-1-4081-4959-1

Hippo
ISBN: HB 978-1-4081-4826-6
PB 978-1-4081-4961-4

Elephant
ISBN: HB 978-1-4081-4827-3
PB 978-1-4081-4958-4